Space for N

The Wildlife Story
of a Donegal Farm

By Liz Sheppard

Drawings by John Shiels
Photographs by Ralph Sheppard

Published in 2011 by Liz Sheppard
Carnowen, Raphoe, Co Donegal, Ireland

A CIP catalogue record for this book is available from the
British Library.

ISBN: 978-0-9570119-0-8

Design and Print by Twist Design, Donegal Town, Co Donegal.

The paper used for this book is FSC-certified.
FSC (the Forest Stewardship Council) promotes the responsible
management of the world's forests.

FSC

The mark of responsible forestry

About the Author

Liz Sheppard grew up on a family farm in East Donegal, and some of her most vivid childhood memories are of long happy hours spent wandering around the lanes and hedgerows and playing on the riverbank, where the world of wildlife was always part of the backdrop.

But life moved on into more urban settings. After the years at college in Derry and Dublin she and her husband, Ralph, spent much of the 1970s in Bristol where they both had teaching posts. Bristol at that time was a great centre for the emerging environmental movement, with many different groups focused on organic growing, wildlife conservation, sustainable lifestyles, anti-nuclear issues – the Sheppards soon found themselves very actively involved.

They always hoped to come back to Ireland however, and Donegal was always beckoning. In 1978 they decided to return to the farm, to take their ideas a stage further and try to put some of them into practice. Over the years they have planted over 25,000 mostly native broadleaf trees, created ponds, monitored bird and plant life, and made detailed surveys of the butterflies and moths on the farm as new habitats emerged. In 2005 their plantations won the RDS/Forest Service Irish Forestry Award for Biodiverse Forest/Woodlands.

In 1988 Liz began writing her popular weekly "Natureview" column in the "Donegal Democrat" in which she often described happenings on the farm, as well as covering a wide range of wildlife, habitat and environment issues across Donegal. A selection of her early articles was published in 1992 as "Donegal for all Seasons". The column continued in the joint "Donegal Democrat" and "Donegal People's Press" until the end of 2008.

"Space for Nature" includes many "Natureview" extracts, woven together with new material to tell the story of developments on the farm over the last thirty years. It's the story of a particular farm – but most of the wildlife characters could turn up in any agricultural part of the Irish countryside. Above all, it's about the constant interest and pleasure to be had by getting closer to the world of nature, and the satisfaction in helping it to feel at home.

Acknowledgements

This book has evolved from a selection of my "Natureview" articles in the "Donegal Democrat" and "Donegal People's Press". I am very grateful to the late Cecil J. King who encouraged me to start writing the column in the "Donegal Democrat" back in 1988, and to subsequent editors of both newspapers who continued their support over two decades.

My sincere thanks are due to Dr Joseph Gallagher, Heritage Officer with Donegal County Council, for his encouragement and his thoughtful and helpful comments on the text. Also to John Shiels for his good-humoured patience and willing co-operation during the production of his fine illustrations. And I would also like to thank Ivan Johnston of Twist Design for his professional and creative work on the lay-out and general design.

The story of the farm and its wildlife has been a big part of the backdrop to my own life, and I am forever grateful to my parents and the previous generations of my family, the Dickeys, who farmed this patch of land for over two centuries, and who played their own various parts in conserving its wildlife value.

Finally, and most of all, I must mention my husband Ralph, the in-house photographer, whose knowledge of the natural world, and enthusiasm for what we have managed to do here, have also made this story possible.

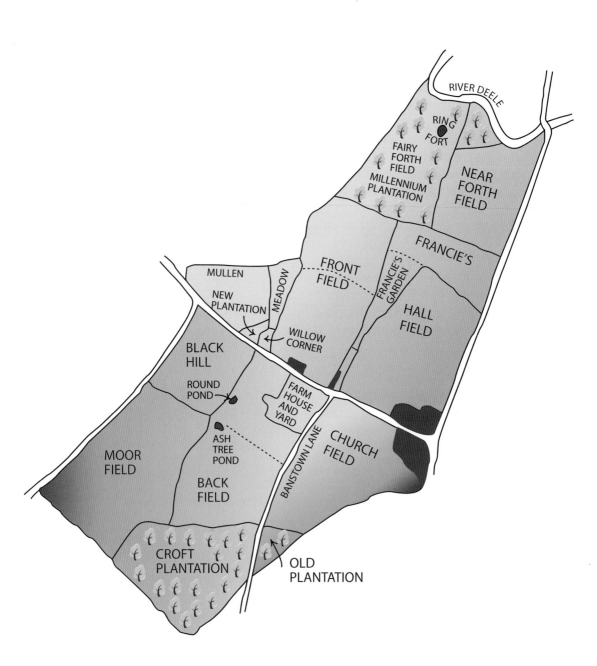

RIVER DEELE

RING FORT

FAIRY FORTH FIELD

MILLENNIUM PLANTATION

NEAR FORTH FIELD

FRANCIE'S

MULLEN

FRONT FIELD

FRANCIE'S GARDEN

MEADOW

NEW PLANTATION

WILLOW CORNER

HALL FIELD

BLACK HILL

ROUND POND

FARM HOUSE AND YARD

ASH TREE POND

BANSTOWN LANE

CHURCH FIELD

MOOR FIELD

BACK FIELD

CROFT PLANTATION

OLD PLANTATION

Contents

Introduction

Having a patch of Earth to look after is a remarkable privilege. My own patch lies in the Deele Valley in East Donegal, an average-sized family farm in a very typical agricultural landscape of rolling hills and sprawling hedgerows. At first glance there doesn't appear to be much in the line of exciting wildlife habitats – but take a closer look at what's going on along the field edges, or sit for a while on the riverbank, and you soon get a sense of the huge community of non-human inhabitants who also think of this patch as home. In fact many of them are very confident that they are its true owners.

When Ralph and I came back to the farm in 1978 after spending the early years of our married life in Bristol, we were keen to discover exactly who our wildlife neighbours were, and to make as much space for them as possible. This is the story of how we have tried to share our patch with these other rightful owners, and the real pleasure and satisfaction that we have had in getting to know them.

Most farms have overgrown corners or damp ditches which have always acted as mini nature reserves. It doesn't take too much effort to protect and extend these, and every improvement of a habitat will draw in a greater diversity of plant and animal life. The vigour and variety of the wildlife community around us is a real measure of the health of the environment we all share. In recent times, high-tech and intensive agriculture has often left little or no space for nature, with clearance and drainage so easily done by ever larger machines, and no consideration for what might be losing its home.

Back in the 1950s when I was growing up here, farming was a very different world. Every farmyard had all kinds of everything, with constant arrivals of baby animals and always something interesting going on in the yard. The summer highlight was the bringing in of the hay – riding out to the field on the empty hay-float and then piling on behind the stack as it was towed into the yard.

Later in the year another great excitement was the arrival of the thresher. All the noise and activity around the big machine – but mainly it was the awful thrill of watching the escaping rats and mice as the stacks were stripped down. In winter the focal point in the yard was the Boiling House where a big boiler cooked potatoes for the pigs and provided an island of warmth for chat and mugs of tea, and a magnet for the dogs and cats. I also remember cosy companionable days in the long byre when the men were making straw ropes – one walking backwards with a winding hook and another deftly feeding in the straw, as in a spinning wheel, until the rope was the full length of the building.

Aaron's Rod

There was often a gang of friends to play with, and the farmyard and fields around had endless possibilities for dens and hide-outs. But I also spent long happy hours on my own, roaming around the countryside with my dog, Nipper, and beginning to discover the world of Nature. In those days birds' nests seemed to be so easy to find! I would bring home tadpoles to watch them develop, catch bumblebees and butterflies in jampots, and gather fistfuls of Marsh Marigolds and Bluebells – long before I learned that wildflowers should be left where they are. I always had the feeling of complete freedom to wander and explore with no sense of anyone being bothered about where I was, the only constraint being the need to be back in time for dinner or tea.

At the age of twelve life changed. I was sent off to boarding school and was soon deep into the whole new world of teenage. Then came the years at college, and city life in Dublin and Bristol, and by the time we moved back to Donegal everything had changed at the farm as well. The milking cows and pigs and hens were all gone, most of the land was being rented out, and just one farm worker remained. Here I was again, back among my lovely familiar fields, with a whole new agenda of green concerns and ideas about living on the land – but with no great master-plan. We would have to let the river flow.

First Things First

Our first autumn back on the farm was a particularly golden one. Every week seemed to produce a fresh mixture of leafy colour and late flowering, and lavish spreads of fruits and berries. As we settled in and began to look into our various options we realized that nothing here would happen very fast, and that choices would not be easy. We had no doubts though about the first thing that we wanted to do. We needed to plant trees. The countryside around was well supplied with mature tree-lined hedgerows but there was very little natural woodland, and hardly an Oak tree in sight. For decades it seemed that the only trees planted by farmers had been dreary lines of Sitka Spruce, grown simply for shelter and speed.

Of course, no plantation even
of broadleaf trees can ever match a native
wood, but if it is made up of native tree
species, at least it will start to attract
the wildlife that depend on those
trees in the complicated web of their
life-cycles. And so we fenced off
one-and-a-half acres of a field corner
and started planting.

The species mix was mostly Oak, Ash
and Birch, with some Alder, Larch and
Spanish Chestnut. There were a few
problems at first with nibbling Hares and
Rabbits, but with improved fencing the trees
soon started to shoot up. Knee-high
became shoulder-high and in about five years we had something like
an overhead canopy. It was great to see the woodland birds gradually
taking possession. Around the sixth summer Willow Warblers, freshly
arrived from Africa, moved straight in to set up territories, two rival
males blasting out their song at one another from opposite ends.
Our woodland had arrived!

Probably the most distinguished visitor in what we now call the Old
Plantation was the Long-eared Owl who used it one summer for his
day-time roost. I was pushing through among the young trees one day
when I was riveted by two huge round eyes staring from the depths
of a Larch tree, literally a few feet from my nose! When startled, a
Long-eared Owl elongates himself into a remarkable thin shape with
raised ear-tufts (which are not ears), imitating a branch. For a couple
of months I often found him in the same tree, and crept around to
view him from different angles, always trying not to waken him.
These remain my best-ever owl encounters.

The River Birds

The lower end of the farm borders on two wide meandering loops of the River Deele, still largely untamed upstream from here, so the water level rises and falls rapidly with changes in rainfall. This particular stretch has good woodland cover along the banks with lots of Alder and Sycamore and some huge Crack Willlows, classic riverbank trees which get their name from their regular habit of splitting and dropping large branches.

Most of the river's inhabitants use the watercourse as a highway and are constantly on the move up and down, so the best way to observe the action is to sit in one spot and wait for the passing traffic. I rarely sit for half-an-hour without some of the water birds putting in an appearance. Maybe a Heron flapping past or a Grey Wagtail flickering yellow along a gravelly edge, or maybe a female Mallard passing with a train of ducklings. It's been sad to notice Moorhens becoming very scarce, probably since the arrival of Mink.

River Deele

The two birds who really catch the spirit of the river are the cocky little Dipper and the dazzling Kingfisher. Dippers tend to occupy the stony upper reaches of a river, and Kingfishers the slower smoother leafy waters further downstream. My local stretch has both types of habitat so I enjoy the company of both birds.

Most Kingfisher sightings are just a turquoise streak zooming past, but now and again one will perch nearby and give a fishing demonstration. It dives in head-first and brings up a small fish, giving it a good hammering on a branch or stone before swallowing it. One memorable summer, the local pair excavated their nest tunnel in the bank just opposite one of my favourite vantage points and I was able to watch them ferrying fish to the nest. Sometimes one had a quick plunge in the water when it came out – apparently the tunnel can become very messy with fish remains so they need to clean themselves.

Dippers are just as fascinating. They often catch my eye with their white bib, bobbing up and down on a stone or along the water's edge. They search for food along the bank but they also feed under water. They swim beneath the surface, using their wings in a sort of slow-motion flight, and they can also walk along the floor of the river, angling themselves very precisely against the flow of the stream to hold their body down. I've often watched one disappearing under and popping up on a stone some distance away. It's a remarkable lifestyle for a songbird – and a Dipper's life is so much part of the river that you will never see one anywhere else.

An Ancient Footway

As a child, this deep old lane was a favourite haunt where we built huts from ferns and played in the stream that crosses at one point under a little stone foot-bridge. Now I know that those ferns come in ten different species, which is a good indicator of the antiquity of the hedge banks that line both sides, and I've discovered that what is known locally as the Banstown Lane is part of a much wider story.

Apparently it was a section of a major bridle-path from Derry which headed on up through the gap at Barnesmore in the Bluestack mountains. In times past people on horseback and pedestrians would have taken the most direct path across the countryside, while carts and carriages might have to follow a more roundabout route. Most bridle-paths have long since been either upgraded into roads, or more often bulldozed away into adjoining fields, but this stretch of about half-a-mile has managed to survive by being a right of way through to another farm. Each year the hedgerows are trimmed back to keep it open and allow for the passage of farm machinery, and this is what has enabled a rich woodland flora to persist.

Another clue to the age of the lane is its depth. In some parts its floor is maybe six feet lower than the fields on either side – simply a result of wear and tear by centuries of foot and hoof. The steep hedge banks are sanctuaries for spring flowers, with different stretches specializing in Primrose or Bluebell or Greater Stitchwort – a flower that better deserves its scientific name "Stellaria", for it comes in wide rambling sheets of white star-like flowers and tiny buds which are a good impersonation of a night sky. In late spring one part of the lane becomes a gorgeous flowery tunnel with billowing lines of Cow Parsley along the sides and an arching canopy of Hawthorn blossom overhead.

Recent research into the Pilgrim Path to Lough Derg has revealed that this bridle-path would have been used by the pilgrims who walked all the way from Derry and Inishowen, and as Lough Derg has been a famous holy place for a thousand years, who knows how many barefoot prayerful souls have passed along this leafy way?

A very Nosey Traveller

Nowadays most of the travellers along the lane are of the non-human variety. One of my most memorable encounters there a few years ago was with a very small one. At first glance it looked like a tiny mouse scuttling about in a wheel rut, but through the binoculars I soon picked up the long snout of a Pygmy Shrew. Shrews belong to a completely different group of mammals from rats and mice which are rodents. They are actually more closely related to Hedgehogs and are known as insectivores, the long-nosed insect-eaters.

When it disappeared into the grass, I put my ear down close beside it and could hear the high-pitched little clicking sound that these creatures make as they search for prey. A Pygmy Shrew is so small that it has to be more or less constantly eating to get enough calories from its food, so its life is basically one long expedition of hunting and munching, day and night, with only short breaks. That long flexible snout fringed with sensitive whiskers is always on the move, searching by touch and smell. It is a strict carnivore, eating almost any creepy-crawly that chances in its path. It must consume twice its bodyweight every day, and will die of starvation if it goes for more than three hours without a meal.

This particular one was so intent on its business that it didn't notice when I parted the grass above it and followed its progress. Slowly I slid my hand just in front of it and held my breath as it walked right on to the palm. It twitched its long nose from side to side as it investigated the seams between my fingers, and continued with the inspection even when I raised it about a foot above the ground. It was a great chance to appreciate its miniscule size. An adult weighs between four and six grams, compared with 24 for the average mouse. The only shrews that I'd seen at such close quarters had been dead ones presented by the cat. Cats don't often consume shrews because of their nasty taste. What a contrast to feel this tiny body literally vibrating with life.

It wasn't long before it decided that my hand hadn't much potential as a hunting ground and it hopped off to find something better. As it went on its way again I could still hear it muttering.

Ferns in the Banstown Lane

Bracken	*Pteridium aquilinum*
Broad Buckler-fern	*Dryopteris dilatata*
Hard Shield-fern	*Polystichum aculeatum*
Hard-fern	*Blechnum spicant*
Hart's-tongue Fern	*Phyllitis scolopendrium*
Lady-fern	*Athyrium filix-femina*
Male-fern	*Dryopteris filix-mas*
Polypody	*Polypodium vulgare*
Scaly Male-fern	*Dryopteris affinis*
Soft Shield-fern	*Polystichum setiferum*

Home help for Long-tailed Tits

T he bird family that I most associate with the lane is the Long-tailed Tit. In winter these travel around in big parties and you can often tune in to their high-pitched "tick-tick" contact call before you see them. Or you notice tiny round balls of feathers with very long tails flitting through the branches. Stand in close to the hedge and they often come right down to within a foot or two of your nose.

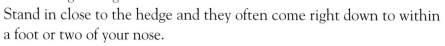

Long-tailed Tits are famous for both the amazing construction of their nest, and their remarkable co-operation when it comes to chick rearing. Some birds, such as Swallows, often have older chicks from an earlier brood helping to feed their younger brothers and sisters later in the summer. But Long-Tailed Tits have taken things a stage further.

In early spring the feeding party begins to break up, with the females moving off to other groups and new females arriving. The males pair up with these new females and each couple goes its separate way and sets about the mammoth task of building the most complicated nest of any Irish bird. The wonderful domed construction is woven from moss and spider web, covered on the outside with pieces of lichen and lined with up to 2000 feathers, and it can expand like elastic to accommodate a growing brood. It takes them three weeks to build.

The sad thing is that many of these masterpieces don't survive. Some are hidden away safely in the thickness of a hedge, but many are set high up in the fork of a tree, in full view of every passing Magpie or Sparrow Hawk, so they don't last long. One that I'd been admiring in the Old Plantation was vandalised and thrown to the ground just a couple of days after I found it. I still have it in a glass jar.

Some bird species would start to build again if their nest was destroyed early in the season, but the single-brooded Long-tails seem to realize that this would take too long, so they decide to put their effort into helping at another nest. But not just any nest! The couple actually splits up and each of them seeks out one of their own brothers and helps to rear his offspring – their nieces and nephews. There's nearly always a nest in the middle of a particularly dense Hawthorn bush along the lane, completely hidden from view – one of the wise ones. This year I watched at least four adults ferrying in the food.

This behaviour is a huge help in raising such large families – sometimes as many as a dozen. The helpers know that they are rearing their own blood-relations, and the following winter when they join up in flocks again, the aunts and uncles remain as part of the family group – a big advantage to any bird which depends on safety in numbers. New angles on the marvellous variety of lifestyle in the bird world are constantly being discovered – but how any researcher managed to get to grips with the Long-tailed Tits is a wonder in itself.

Pond life back in business

Another valuable habitat which has vanished in most agricultural areas is the farmyard pond. In this locality there also used to be lots of well-constructed flax dams, where the flax crop had to be soaked for a couple of weeks after it was pulled. When flax growing faded away around the 1950s the dams soon filled up with vegetation, but traces of them are not hard to find, and if you want to make a pond they are obvious spots to choose.

It took just a day with a digger to transform the couple of old dam sites in our Back Field into two nice little expanses of water, each one around 150 square yards. And during the following summer it was remarkable how quickly a whole pond community built up again.

These inhabitants are a weird and wonderful lot, mostly very small and all highly specialised. There's something fascinating about this mini water-world, confined to a small area, and so distinct from the habitats around it. The first thing to catch the eye is usually the Whirligig Beetles, tiny black and silver beads zooming around in circles on the surface like dodgems, investigating everything that lands on the water. One will push around an insect with its nose with several other Whirligigs in hot pursuit. They are so highly tuned to living on the surface that their eyes are divided horizontally – the top half adapted for seeing in air and the lower half for under water.

Also on the surface you find the Pond Skaters which are actually walking on the water, using the furry pads on four of their feet. Just under the surface you often see Water Boatmen (or Backswimmers) swimming along upside-down, with two long legs stretching out sideways like paddles. There are several types of water beetle, from tiny pinheads up to the Great Diving Beetle at about 3cm long, all easy to detect as they have to come up regularly to collect an air supply at the surface.

Down on the pond floor there are slow movers like the water snails and flatworms, and big numbers of little Freshwater Shrimps which often swim around in pairs, clutched together in their mating process which lasts for several days. There are lots of insect nymphs and larvae, including the famous Caddis Fly larva which constructs a protective coat for itself from little pebbles and vegetation and anything it can find, so each outfit is unique. It moves around with just the head and front feet sticking out.

In early spring the big drama is the frog mating party which can go on for several days. And then there's the anxious watch over the frogspawn as the black dots slowly turn into commas, and eventually hatch out into what seems like millions of tadpoles. These are high on the menu of many other pond dwellers and the numbers dwindle fast, and there's usually just a few who survive long enough to sit out on the duckweed as tiny froglets. Seeing them slowly struggling towards life beyond the pond is like watching the first prehistoric life emerging from the waters!

On sunny summer days the pond edge is flickering with dazzling little damselflies – Large Red, Blue-tailed and Common Blue, and sometimes one of their larger dragonfly relations puts in an appearance. Dragon and damselfly nymphs are fierce-looking creatures with upturned tails which can spend three or four years underwater, while the flashy adult forms live for only about a month.

Water Mint, Starwort & Pondweed

As well as all this action and interest, the ponds also add a whole extra dimension to the atmosphere of my Back Field. Reflecting the light and colour of the sky and the moving clouds, or rippling in the wind – there's a great sense of peace and contemplation to be enjoyed beside even a small stretch of still water. Once, when it happened to be at just the right angle, I caught the reflection of the full Moon.

The Atlantic Connection

Every few years the ponds need to have a spring clean. Silt and vegetation have built up again and the digger has to be called in to scoop out the pond floor. One year as I was watching this process I was amazed to see a large Eel, about a metre long, dislodged from the mud. It made a very quick get-away, slithering off into the little stream that feeds the pond. Several other smaller ones were revealed that same day.

Eels have a most extraordinary life story. They are all born in a deep part of the South-west Atlantic known as the Sargasso Sea. This is the breeding ground for both European and American Eels, but when the larvae hatch out they move off in opposite directions. American larvae mature quickly as they don't have far to go, but the European ones take nearly three years to drift right across the Atlantic, by which time they have developed into Elvers.

Once they taste fresh water they start looking for a home. Some remain around estuaries and coastal areas but many move up rivers and into lakes, and some travel far upstream to find a quiet spot in some remote ditch or pond. Females tend to travel further inland than males, and they also live longer and grow much larger, often to well over a metre. My Back Field ponds are obviously a very suitable habitat, but I'm still intrigued by the thought of such huge creatures lurking there, and how they manage to scrape a living is certainly a puzzle.

Eventually, after as long as 20 years, the Eel gets the urge to reproduce. It changes from greenish-brown into its silver breeding dress and sets off on the incredible return journey to its birthplace. At this stage of its life it doesn't stop to feed. It finds its way along watercourses, travelling overland if necessary on wet nights, and when it reaches the coast it heads off west into the ocean. How could they ever have evolved such a lengthy migration route? One theory is that this behaviour pattern developed when the two continents were much closer to one another, and as they drifted apart the Eels gradually elongated their journey, and accordingly lengthened the time spent in their saltwater larval stage.

It takes about six months to reach their destination, and in the depths of the ocean the eggs are laid and fertilized. Each female can produce up to 20 million eggs. When the job is done, the adults are never seen again.

The African Connection

The African connection is a much more obvious one, celebrated every spring with the arrival of the migrant birds. It's a long time now since Corncrakes have been heard in this locality, but around ten years ago there was suddenly a new voice in the summer chorus, and it's a particularly melodious one.

Blackcaps used to be known only as occasional migrants in winter, famous for their aggressive behaviour around bird tables. I've seen one take possession of one of my peanut feeders, and no one else got a look-in for at least a week. But most birds don't sing in the middle of winter so Blackcap song was never heard, so when it started to echo around the countryside in spring it was obvious that something new was happening. It turns out that the winter birds are part of a population that breeds in Central Europe, while most of the summer birds come up from Africa in the normal way of warblers. The two other warblers that I hear around the farm are Chiffchaff and Willow Warbler, and it's remarkable how the three species turn up within just a day or two of one another every year, in late March or early April. For the following three months their three distinct songs make up a big part of the summer soundtrack.

Shortly after the warblers have settled in, the red-letter day in the yard comes with the arrival of the first Swallow. We often have up to half a dozen pairs nesting inside the old sheds, using the same beams and ledges year after year, obviously coming from many generations of the same families. I can't imagine a summer without those dark arrows constantly darting around my air-space, zooming in and out of buildings, and their cheerful chatter as they sit up on the overhead wires.

But the final visitor to arrive is the one
I'm always most anxious about. Spotted
Flycatchers don't have the high profile
of Swallows, or a distinctive song like
the warblers, and although they're quite
common around here, many people have
never even heard of them. And that
always surprises me for when you get to
know these birds, you wonder how you
never noticed them before.

Spotted Flycatcher

In my garden they've been around since I
first became aware of birds, and probably long
before. They love to nest in creepers and ivy, and a pair has always
nested near one particular window on the front of the house. When
the ageing Virginia Creeper eventually died off one year, we put up a
nest box specially designed for Flycatchers, with a half-open front, in
good time for their arrival the following spring. I was really thrilled
when a pair moved straight into it the very day they arrived!
The creeper is now well grown again, but the Flycatchers are still
using the box.

These are quirky characters with very eye-catching behaviour. Each
one has a few favourite look-out perches, usually in full view, and it
dives out again and again from the same spot to snatch insects, and
very rarely misses. They do all sorts of fancy aerial manoeuvres,
hovering and plunging and even flitting after butterflies. They can
take items as large as a dragonfly, and can remove the sting of a bee or
wasp by bashing it against a branch. As well as the pair in the box, I
always have one or two other pairs nesting around the garden and it's a
delight to sit and watch their antics on summer evenings. I can even
hear the little snap of their beaks as they make a catch.

Spotted Flycatchers have disappeared from many parts of Britain where
they used to be common, and there's some evidence that their numbers
may be falling in Ireland, which makes me all the more delighted when
they turn up safely again every May.

The Croft Plantation

By 1990 we reckoned that the time had come to take the plunge with a larger plantation. Our earlier efforts had worked so well, with many of the trees reaching up to around thirty feet, that we decided to devote the whole of a 10-acre field, known as the Upper Croft, to the new woodland.

This was in a different league altogether, with 12,000 trees to play around with, and all sorts of possible combinations and designs. We decided against any sort of mechanized ridge planting which would have left a very unpleasant corrugated surface, and insisted on every tree being dug in by spade and foot to create a nice level woodland floor.

We divided the field into eight sections, marked out by irregular winding paths, and planted each one with three different species. Again we went for mostly native trees, with big numbers of Oak, Ash, Cherry, Alder and Birch. We included some Norway Maple, Small-leafed Lime and Spanish Chestnut which are not Irish natives but are not far from their natural European range, and have particularly useful timber. We also put in some Scots Pine, as a native conifer, and some Southern Beech from South America which has a good reputation for supporting wildlife variety. In two of the sections, the broadleaf trees were interplanted with Lodgepole Pine (non-native) which were removed after six or seven years and sold as Christmas trees. This left wider spacing between the broadleafs than in other sections, making thinning somewhat easier.

Almost twenty years old now, the Croft Plantation has been a real delight at every stage of growth along the way. It didn't take long for the local wildlife to discover a new habitat. The most surprising thing the first summer was how quickly the bare earth, in what had been a potato field the previous year, became covered in a rich sward of grass. It came from nowhere! We had to do a fair amount of trampling and weeding to make sure the young trees didn't get swamped.

For the first year of two, in what was basically a wild grassland habitat, we had Reed Buntings and Meadow Pipits in summer and a large number of Snipe in winter – none of these being at all common in this locality. After five or six years we had a few summers of Sedge and Grasshopper Warblers, but as the trees grew up and the woodland birds took over, all of these more temporary species dwindled away. But by then it was becoming a real woodland scene, with new arrivals and discoveries every year, and an ever-changing atmosphere with the flow of the seasons. It's where I've had some of my most memorable wildlife highlights over the years, and it's still coming up with surprises.

Dazzled by Gold Swifts

One of my most magical chance encounters happened one evening along one of the plantation paths. About fifty Gold Swift moths were all putting on their remarkable courtship display, each one swinging back and forth like a small pendulum, with the shining gold spangles on their wings glinting in the golden light of the sunset.

These moths are fairly widespread in Donegal but are normally seen in much smaller numbers, and nearer dusk. This particular evening was warm and still, with such perfect conditions for Gold Swifts that a big number of them decided that it was time for their Big Night.

Moths have a great variety of lifestyles, and Gold Swifts spend most of their existence as caterpillars, living underground and feeding on plant roots. After two years they develop into pupae, and when they eventually emerge from the ground, they have just one thing on their mind – finding a mate and setting up the next generation. Many moths feed on nectar and plant juices but Gold Swifts don't have any mouth-parts in their adult form, so their short life on the wing is all about sex. Moths attract a partner by giving off a strong scent which can travel downwind for half-a-mile, and with most of them it's the female that sends out the signal. But in Gold Swift courtship the male produces the scent as he performs his pendulum dance, and the females don't take long to get the message. As I watched the display of flickering gold, couples began to link up and slip in under the leaves, and after about fifteen minutes most of them had found a partner. Once the job is done they survive for just a few days.

Gold Swift

The Moth Trap

Lunar Thorn…Rosy Rustic…Clouded Silver…Brussels Lace…
Powdered Quaker…Beautiful Snout…Pink-barred Sallow…
Brindled Pug… These are just a few of the other amazing
moth characters that inhabit the farm. The names give some idea of
their subtle shapes and shades and patterns, some as brightly coloured
as butterflies and others with extremely crafty camouflages to blend
with different backgrounds. As well as their variety of lifestyle the
various species appear at different times of the year, sometimes on
very precise dates, and they use different caterpillar foodplants and
different habitats. They form the links in many foodchains and
wildlife webs, and are a great illustration of how Nature takes every
opportunity to fill up every available niche. They are also a good
yardstick for measuring biodiversity and the health of the
environment, and studying their population changes over time can
warn of possible problems. It was obvious that we would want to
find out how many of them were sharing our patch.

Brimstone Moth

Buff-tip

So about fifteen years ago we got our first moth trap and Ralph started to immerse himself in moth identification books, and the picture which has been building up ever since has been a real eye-opener. A moth trap is simply a metal or plastic container with an ultraviolet light fixed on top to attract the moths, and a funnel to encourage them to fall inside. Here they settle down among a pile of egg cartons and when we take these out in the morning, some of them fly off to the nearest vegetation, but most sit tight while they are checked out and recorded and don't take off again until nightfall.

Merveille du Jour

Pink-barred Sallow

Opening up the trap in the morning is like a lucky dip. On a good night in summer, hazy and warm, we might have 400 individuals of 50 species in our back garden. We're still turning up an occasional one that we haven't seen here before. The largest one that we catch is the Poplar Hawk-moth, with sculpted wings spanning over three inches, held out at different angles to look like dead leaves. There's the gaudy Garden Tiger in orange, brown and cream, and the cool green Large Emerald with wavy white lines. Several come in tones of yellow and tan, like the Brimstone and Scalloped Oak, and the Carpet group have a whole variety of beautiful patterns like Persian rugs. Some have shiny gold spangles and spots, and the Burnished Brass is a striking iridescent green.

Two I always look out for are the brightly speckled Magpie Moth, and the Peach Blossom which has markings like pink petals to match the Bramble flowers where it lays its eggs. The Feathered Thorn has huge feathered antennae, and the Snout has a long nose and delta wings which make it look like a Concorde aircraft. The Flame, Buff-tip and Red Sword-grass look just like bits of broken twig, and others have the exact colouring of the background that they rest on. When the Peppered Moth lands on Birch bark, or the Merveille du Jour among lichens, they simply disappear!

So far, we have recorded over 250 different species of macro-moth on the farm. Ralph has also been involved in trapping widely across Donegal and the grand total for the county has reached almost 400 – out of something like 500 species for the whole of Ireland. The Donegal Moth website has pictures and distribution maps of all the Donegal species. There are also well over a thousand micro-moth species in the country – the next challenge.

Night-World
of the Badger

Long warm summer evenings, at around nine or ten o'clock, are some of my favourite times for going on the prowl. Moving along the hedgerows past whiffs of Elderflower and Honeysuckle as the whole night-world is beginning to come awake, there's always an air of excitement about what might appear.

Some of the best late entertainment has always been provided by the Badgers. The sett that I watch most often is usually occupied by one female and her two or three cubs, and their evening appearances are fairly reliable. Sometimes the mother is first to emerge, raising her snout high to sniff the air, and if she catches my scent when I'm upwind of her she may shoot straight in again. At other times the cubs are already out by the time I arrive and I can hear their squeaks and squeals from quite a distance. They're often so caught up in their rough and tumble games that they can chase one another to within a few feet of me without realizing that I'm there. They have sharp senses of smell and hearing, but fairly poor eyesight.

Honeysuckle

A well-established badger sett is like an ancient fortress. It generally has a substantial network of underground tunnels and chambers, with several separate entrances, and the extent of the excavation underneath is reflected in the size of the earthworks on top. Each extended family usually has a main sett, with several other outposts within their territory which they may occupy at different times.

Some evenings the atmosphere around the sett is very relaxed and they sit about, having lengthy scratching sessions and communing with one another. I've watched a mating pair in action for at least half an hour. They are very fastidious house- keepers, regularly changing their bedding, and it's fascinating to watch one deftly rolling up a bundle of grass while it travels backwards towards the sett at remarkable speed.

On other evenings they seem to have a great sense of urgency to be somewhere else, and they move off immediately on their night-time patrols along well-worn trails. Their highly organized world has a timeless quality about it, confident and contented, and I always feel heartened by glimpses of it. One very surprising glimpse that I had not long ago was as I approached the sett and could hear the racket of the young ones playing. But when a pair of them tumbled out in front of me, it was actually a young Badger and a young Fox.
The Fox cub had apparently dropped by for a game.

Return of the Buzzards

Around 1990 there was a dramatic new presence in the skies over Donegal. The Buzzards were back. Like Eagles, Buzzards were shot and poisoned into extinction in Ireland, and their last breeding record in Donegal had been in 1883. In 1933 a pair bred in Antrim, but it wasn't until 1966 that they really got going again, with seven pairs nesting on Rathlin Island, and from there they started a steady spread across the country. They're now well established north-east of a line from Sligo to Cork.

I had come across a few of them in border areas but it was still a big surprise when I first saw them soaring high above my garden. I was idly watching the Swallows whirling around the tree-tops when suddenly my eye was riveted by two huge dark shapes much further up, slowly circling on motionless wings against a clear blue sky. The long broad wings could only belong to one of the larger birds of prey.

Nowadays they've become very much part of the local scene. They're quite noisy birds and I can pick up their shrill ringing call from inside the house, even when they're flying far above. For a few years a pair has nested in a little group of Ash trees in the Back Field and I often see them wheeling and gliding together, or I come across one of them sitting up on a tall tree or ESB pole, on the look-out for prey. They will eat almost any small animal or bird and any sort of carrion, but on the odd occasion when I've seen one with a catch, it has always been a young Magpie. But they're not too proud to cash in on grubs and worms when they get the chance, and just after the field has been cut for silage they're often down on the ground, pacing around to pick up small items and taking short flights to pounce on something. They look so comical and ungainly on their feet, compared with their easy grace and power in the air.

It's great to see these magnificent birds finding their rightful place again in the wildlife web. As they spread to new areas many people are seeing this large raptor for the first time – about four times as heavy as a Sparrowhawk – and assume that they're looking at an Eagle. And of course in Donegal, with the ongoing success of the Golden Eagle Re-introduction Project since 2001, people are getting much more tuned in to birds of prey. But Eagles are in a different league again – about four times the weight of a Buzzard and with twice the wingspan! And Eagles are almost always seen in unfenced upland areas while Buzzards favour farmland with good mature trees. If an Eagle ever passes this way, I'm sure it won't be hanging around for long.

Super-Grass

The Back Field with its ponds and Ash trees and nesting Buzzards is what lies between the garden and the Croft Plantation. It hasn't been ploughed up for many years and in recent times has had no grazing animals, being cut just twice a year for silage. We keep a pathway open through the long grass by trimming it regularly with a run of the lawnmower, and this shows up as a winding green snake across the field. Early on it was christened "the Yellow Brick Road" and the name has stuck.

One of the most striking things about old grassland like this is the rich variety among the grasses themselves. What appear to be greenish seed-heads are actually the grasses in full flower, each head made up of tiny spikelets, in all sorts of patterns and textures. Some are light-headed and feathery like the Fescues and Bents; others are more solid and symmetrical such as Timothy, Crested Dogstail and Meadow Foxtail. Some have thin wiry stems while others are more succulent. Cocksfoot has chunky clusters of spikelets and the Rye grasses have them neatly arranged on alternate sides of the stem.

My favourite is Yorkshire Fog, soft and silky, with fine hair all over its leaves. It starts out pale pink and develops through dusky purple to end up with creamy-white seed-heads. It's a great one for flower arrangements. Sweet Vernal Grass has inconspicuous wispy flower-heads, but is well known for its powerful scent, which gives that lovely summery smell to a new-mown field.

Yorkshire Fog

Hawthorn Blossom

As well as the interest of the grasses, the field has its seasonal run of wildflowers, with carpets of Dandelion yellow or Cuckoo-flower purple. In a so-called "improved" grassland these would be banished as weeds, but wild plants like these can create a herb-rich sward which makes excellent silage, especially appreciated by horses.

It's also much appreciated by the grassland butterflies. There are no great rarities in this part of the county, but we get good numbers of Meadow Browns and Ringlets, an occasional Small Heath or Small Copper, and at the peak of their season the whole field can be flickering with Green-veined Whites. But the biggest butterfly spectacle happened one year towards the end of September, and although it wasn't all my doing, I like to think I had a bit of a hand in it.

Grasses in the Back Field

Cock's-foot	*Dactylis glomerata*
Common Bent	*Agrostis capillaris*
Creeping Soft-grass	*Holcus mollis*
Crested Dog's-tail	*Cynosurus cristatus*
Marsh Foxtail	*Alopecurus geniculatus*
Meadow Foxtail	*Alopecurus pratensis*
Perennial Rye-grass	*Lolium perenne*
Rough Meadow-grass	*Poa trivialis*
Sweet Vernal-grass	*Anthoxanthum odoratum*
Timothy	*Phleum pratense*
Yorkshire-fog	*Holcus lanatus*

Cuckoo Flower and Dandelion

The Caterpillar
Rescue Mission

Small Tortoiseshells are one of the beautiful colourful Vanessid butterflies that lay their eggs exclusively on nettles. There are lots of nice healthy nettles around the edges of the Back Field, but that summer they homed in instead on a few clumps right out in the middle. Many hundreds of caterpillars hatched out, swarming over the nettle tops so that some of them looked completely black from a distance, but as the date for silage cutting was getting close, they were all doomed to a sticky ending. I decided that a rescue mission was called for, so I filled a basket with caterpillar-laden nettles and moved the lot to safe locations around the field edge.

Small Tortoiseshell

Over the next three weeks or so I kept a close eye on what were now "my" caterpillars, and watched them thrive and grow and spread out through the nettle beds. They also dwindled fast in number. Some would have been eaten by birds, but their big enemy was wasps. I was fascinated to watch groups of caterpillars doing a strange head-waving movement, all in unison, when a wasp came near, to try to scare it off. And I came across a wasp in the very act of snatching a small caterpillar and carrying it to the ground where it killed the victim by stinging.

But the caterpillars that survived were soon too big for a wasp to handle, and by the end of August they were starting to turn into pupae. This is the amazing stage of butterfly development where the caterpillar attaches itself to one spot, shrinks in size and develops a hard skin. Inside the skin, all the body tissues melt down and rearrange themselves into the adult insect, which eventually bursts out from its hard case. The first pupa that I discovered was a real surprise because I didn't know that pupae are able to move. It was a completely still day and I noticed that one nettle was shaking – strongly enough to quiver all the nettles around it. When I looked closer, I found the pupa hanging from the stem by one very fine point, twitching and gyrating enough to cause all the movement. There was a tiny black insect sitting on it, and apparently this twitching is another defense tactic to shake off ichneumon wasps which act as parasites on the pupa.

Another day I noticed a large caterpillar hanging by its tail with head curled up, and the next day it had turned into a nice fresh pupa, speckled with gold. A few days later after a stormy night I found that its nettle had been flattened to the ground, so I brought it into the house where the pupa developed safely in the kitchen, and hatched into a perfect butterfly exactly 18 days after I first found it.

The following day I took it back to the field where big numbers of its relations were now also on the wing. The next couple of weeks were warm and bright and every blink of sunlight had them out basking on a convenient late crop of dandelions. The highest number that I counted at any one time was 92 – the largest gathering of Small Tortoiseshells that I've ever seen.

Small Tortoiseshell – pupa

Butterflies found on the Farm

Green Hairstreak	*Callophrys rubi*
Green-veined White	*Pieris napi*
Large White	*Pieris brassicae*
Meadow Brown	*Maniola jurtina*
Orange Tip	*Anthocharis cardamines*
Painted Lady	*Vanessa cardui*
Peacock	*Inachis io*
Red Admiral	*Vanessa atalanta*
Ringlet	*Aphantopus hyperantus*
Small Copper	*Lycaena phlaeas*
Small Heath	*Coenonympha pamphilus*
Small Tortoiseshell	*Aglais urticae*
Small White	*Pieris rapae*
Speckled Wood	*Pararge aegeria*

The Millennium Plantation

By the time the Millennium came round there was a lot of talk about tree planting, and it seemed an obvious time to put in another plantation. The two earlier ones had been started in 1980 and 1990 so keeping up the sequence at 10-year intervals would give a good comparison between the different ages and stages of development. By then the broadleaf planting grants were much improved, and we were keen to try out some new ideas and do things a bit differently from in the Croft.

We chose another 10-acre field, known as the Fairy Forth, right at the other end of the farm along the river bank. As its name suggests, it already had an oasis of Hawthorn, Blackthorn and Gorse bushes crowning a sizeable rocky outcrop in the middle of it. This was marked as a Fort on the first edition of the OS map, and is listed as a Ringfort in the "Archaeological Survey of Ireland".

Blackthorn and Gorse

This time we decided to go for all native Irish trees – Oak, Ash, Rowan, Willow, Alder, Elder, Aspen, Scots Pine, Birch, Hazel, Cherry and Crab Apple. And we were pleased to be able to get most of them from stock grown from Irish seed. They were planted in little groups of 30 or 40 trees of one species all together, which is supposed to give a better rate of growth – rather than the mixture of three species in each section that we have in the Croft. And most important, we devised a way of spacing the trees while planting, which gave the correct density per acre but avoided them ending up in long straight lines. This will eventually give a more natural feel to the growing woodland.

The planting was completed during the autumn of 1999 and the final Oak was scheduled to be set in place on Millennium Eve. A hole was prepared at the chosen spot, and several friends joined us for the occasion, complete with a bottle of champagne and a large candle. We took an alarm clock to the field to make sure that the deed was done on the very stroke of midnight! But of course we didn't need the clock - for right on cue, the sky around the whole valley was lit up with fireworks.

The Millennium Oak now stands in the middle of a little clearing in the wood surrounded by a ring of Cherry trees, while the Thorn bush outcrop remains as another prominent focal point. As an archaeological site, this had to have a 15-metre margin all around it left unplanted, which has become a sunny sheltered sanctuary for plant and insect life. In both of the large plantations we are trying to maintain the pathways and small clearings to allow in enough light for a varied flora to develop. On a bright summer day almost every pool of sunlight is being patrolled by a Speckled Wood butterfly.

Young Birch

Millennium Planation Edge

Looking an Otter
in the Eye

Having a new woodland at the lower end of the farm has certainly added a whole new dimension to walks to the river. But the river itself is still the big attraction. When I'm out and about on early summer mornings I usually find myself drawn in that direction, and make time to sit for a while in the hope of seeing an Otter. Dippers and Kingfishers are always a delight, but an otter sighting is the icing on the cake.

This doesn't happen very often – maybe only once in a year – for these are elusive animals and largely nocturnal, although on quiet stretches of river like this one, they can appear at any time of day. I've sometimes been surprised by one approaching quite noisily through the bank vegetation, or doing a lot of splashing while chasing fish, but usually it's a silent sinuous body slithering along the edge or arching and looping through the water.

On one memorable occasion one of them came close enough to look me in the eye! I'd been watching it about fifty metres downstream, moving about in a deep pool, now and again sticking up its long pointed tail at odd angles as it chased fish. As it started to work its way up towards me, I knew it would have to surface where the river gets shallow and stony, and I froze every muscle as it came out into full view. Right beside me now, at just a couple of metres, the Otter suddenly froze as well and sat up to stare at me for several seconds. I thought that it would make a quick getaway, but no, it moved on quite unconcerned into deeper water, fished up an eel and sat out on the bank, holding it in its front paws and munching through it in leisurely fashion. Finally it disappeared upstream, travelling under water again, leaving a tell-tale trail of silvery bubbles.

Back in the 1990s I would often come across Mink around the river, sometimes a whole family of them, but nowadays they are much less frequent. When these sharp little creatures first started to spread through the countryside after escaping from fur farms, there was a lot of concern that they would upset the natural balance and cause harm to other wildlife, even competing with the native Otter. But although they have certainly damaged some bird populations, it seems that their numbers have stabilized by now, and the Otters don't appear to have been greatly bothered. And even though I'm very aware that the Mink

Deele Riverbank

shouldn't be here at all, I must admit that I do enjoy watching them now and again. I once saw a couple of young ones having great fun in a fallen tree on the river bank, chasing one another through the branches as nimble as squirrels, and then slipping into the water to continue the game, swimming around after one another, nose to tail.

The Pigeon Family

Most old farmyards had a collection of pigeon-holes in one of the buildings, and pigeon pie would always have been a handy standby. In our yard there was a long row of them along the stable loft, and even though these were blocked up many years ago, the descendants of their tenants are still around – up to half-a-dozen of them often sitting up on the rooftops or roosting inside some of the old outhouses, as relaxed and companionable as their city cousins.

These domestic or feral pigeons come in a whole range of colours – combinations of light and dark grey, cinnamon and white, some all dark and some pure white. But all of them are descended from the native Rock Dove which is a wild and wary bird, found around remote cliffs and headlands along the north and west coasts. A couple of my current yard pigeons have markings very well matched to their wild ancestor – with two clear black wing-stripes.

As on most farms, we also have plenty of Woodpigeons. These are larger plumper birds and so common that they often go unnoticed, but if you can catch that stylish plumage in the sunlight, it's worth getting out the binoculars! Shaded pinkish-purple on the breast through to blue-grey on the head, with a lovely glint of green and violet above the white neck-patch.

Now and again we're pleased to have a pair of Stock Doves, which are getting fairly scarce in Donegal with the move away from arable farming. And in recent years we've had a pair of Collared Doves nesting near the house – smaller sandy-coloured birds with a neat black neck-collar. These hit the headlines back in the 1960s when they colonised the whole country within a few years of their first appearance in Ireland in 1959. It was part of a great population explosion which spread out from their original homeland in India, and swept across Europe in a couple of decades.

All members of the pigeon family have a remarkable ability which helps them to fast-track the rearing of their young. Both male and female produce a thick cheesy mixture known as pigeon milk from glands inside the crop, and feed it neat to their chicks for the first three or four days after hatching, mixed after that with increasing amounts of their normal food. No other Irish birds do this – only Penguins and Flamingos do something similar. It gives the chicks a great start in life and they develop much quicker than other birds of similar size.

I'm probably most aware of my pigeon neighbours on spring mornings when I wake up to the dawn chorus and they are usually in full voice. Each of the species has its distinctive pattern of "coos", repeated again and again like a mantra. And the Woodpigeons in particular keep up their calling well on into the summer, long after most other birds have relaxed their efforts.

A Good Word for the Magpie

"Mag" was an old word for someone who was a bit too chatty and gossipy, and "pie" is another form of "pied", meaning black and white. Put the two words together and you have a neat description of a noisy black-and-white chatterbox. The Magpie has always been famous for its cheeky behaviour, but I've often wondered why the sight of a single Magpie came to be so feared as a sign of bad luck, especially as higher numbers of them were reckoned to forecast all kinds of good fortune. There are many versions of the well-known rhyme, but they all start off with "one for sorrow".

Whatever about the superstitions, Magpies are often accused of having thieving habits and get blamed for robbing songbird nests. But their bad name is really not deserved. They do get attracted by bright objects and sometimes take them back to the nest, but they don't go around searching for them! And they do take eggs and nestlings if they get the chance, but there are many other nest robbers on the job as well – Cats, Rats, Stoats and Sparrowhawks are far more stealthy, so the rowdy Magpie gets blamed for more than its fair share of plundering.

There has been plenty of research which shows that where Magpie numbers are highest, the local songbird populations are also at their most healthy and stable. On the farm here I'm likely to see a Magpie on almost any walk and there are often one or two strutting about the garden, but over the years the populations of neither Magpies nor local songbirds seem much changed. What has most control over bird numbers is the amount of food available to them in winter, and predators are just creaming off the surplus. In their normal habitat of woodland and open countryside, the Magpie will be playing its proper role in keeping Nature's balance.

In any case, Magpies are great entertainment. They have a very comical way of hopping sideways when something catches their eye, and as with the Woodpigeon, it's worth taking a closer look at that handsome plumage. The black parts show up with beautiful sheens of purple on the head, blue and green on the wings, and green and bronze on the tail – a real flashy character in fact! The bird scene would certainly be a lot less glamorous without them, but the other members of the Crow family that inhabit the farm are just as interesting.

The Canny Crows

You never travel very far through the countryside without coming across a member of the Crow family. In general, they're reckoned to be the most intelligent of all the birds, and in evolutionary terms, some of the most advanced. In Ireland we have seven resident crow species, and six of those are found on the farm, the only exception being the Chough, a rare speciality of the remotest fringes of the Donegal coast.

At the other end of the scale, Jackdaws turn up everywhere. We have an extended family of them living around the yard and garden who use the same nest sites year after year, never giving up hope of breaking through the wire defences on the chimney pots, and occasionally succeeding. Some of these certainly seem to be slow learners, for there's a high ledge in the gable of the barn where they constantly try to build, and never manage it. The twigs fall through and pile up on the floor inside in a pyramid that can almost reach the roof – a great source of kindling for the fire! We recently filled 25 sacks.

But there's one Jackdaw character who has all his wits about him, and has been occupying a prime site under the eaves for at least six years. He's easily identified by his deformed beak which has an upper mandible shaped like a long pointed hook,

Jay

protruding by about an inch, so that he has to hold his head sideways to pick up things from the ground. Far from being a handicap, it seems that this is a useful weapon, for he sees off anyone who tries to oust him from his abode, and he's always the first taker when a supply of titbits appears.

Rooks nest in big communal rookeries, and we don't have one of these raucous bird cities anywhere on the farm, although plenty of them feed around the fields. But it's during the winter that we most enjoy the spectacle of their comings and goings. There's a huge and long-established night-time roost about two miles away, and one of their flight-paths passes over here as regularly as clockwork, fanning out every morning after dawn and returning at twilight. The flocks have both Rooks and Jackdaws, and many hundreds of them stream past in ten or fifteen minutes. You can detect the high-pitched chatter of the Jackdaws, compared with the deep caws of the Rooks – the classic sound-track of a late winter afternoon. Hooded Crows assemble at smaller winter roosts, and in the last couple of years a flock of about a hundred has regularly gathered in the Croft Plantation.

Magpies and Hooded Crows tend to keep a low profile during the breeding season and their nests are usually well-hidden in good cover. And just occasionally we've also had a pair of Ravens, with a nest in one of the very tallest trees. These are the giants of the Crow family – at over two feet long, they're two or three times as big as a Rook. They're also reckoned to be the brainiest of all, and since ancient times the Raven has been seen as a special bird, a symbol of wisdom and power, sometimes with a hint of danger. The Druids believed that they could detect 64 distinct Raven calls and sounds, all with different meanings, and used them for predicting the future. In more recent times, researchers have been working out the meanings of the various calls, such as contact-calls, display-calls, protest-calls and threat-calls, and are discovering a very complex communication system. The only call that I recognize is the deep "prok-prok" which is their real trademark, and I'm always pleased to hear it passing by, for Ravens are largely birds of the uplands and not too common in this locality.

Marsh Marigolds

Even more exciting though was another arrival on the scene that was completely unexpected. The Jay is the crow that comes in technicolour – pink, black and white, with a bright flash of blue on the wing. These were well-known in the south of the country, but had hardly ever been seen in the north-west until around 1980. Gradually they started to appear in the best of Donegal's oakwoods, and then began to spread into generally wooded areas, but I'd never seen one around here. And then one day, in the autumn of 2003, I was walking through the Croft Plantation when a harsh loud call sounded right above me, and out it flew. It perched just a couple of metres ahead, giving me a fantastic view. Through most of that winter we had about a dozen of them, a remarkable gathering. In most winters since then, we've usually had two or three.

Jays are essentially woodland birds, and their discovery of the plantation seemed to show that it had moved up into a new league.

The Wildflower Meadow

Wildflowers around the farm generally have to find a home along the field edges. The best spots would include some of the remaining Primrose and Bluebell banks, and the sheets of Wood Anemone and Wild Garlic along the river. But we do have one sheltered acre where the flowers have been largely left to do their own thing, in a damp and undrainable corner which has always been known as the Meadow.

One side of this narrow little field is bordered by an overgrown hedge of Hawthorn and Aspen, and the other side has an ancient "double ditch" with a classic woodland flora – Bluebell and Pignut and the farm's only Early Purple Orchids. At the lower end, the hedge has a few fine Holly trees and a large clump of Gorse bushes, and at the upper end we've planted a little group of different Willow species along with a few Aspens.

Meadow Sweet and Purple Loosestrife

In spring and early summer it flushes yellow with Meadow Buttercups in the drier spots and Marsh Marigolds in the damper ones. And there's an elegant line of Flag Irises along the lower hedge and ditch. June and July bring good numbers of Common Spotted Orchids – again the only corner of the farm where these lovely frilly flowers still survive. All orchids are very choosy about where they grow, and turn up in only the best natural habitats. Many of them are now under pressure and dwindling in number. They have highly specialised lifestyles, and the little florets come in a big variety of subtle and elaborate designs to attract different insects. Each orchid species depends on a particular fungus in the soil to enable it to develop. They produce masses of tiny seeds like dust, which can blow for miles and which have no internal food-store of their own, unlike most other seeds. Under ground the seed and fungus team up together, living off one another. The fungus grows more in winter and the orchid seed gathers strength in summer, and after between four and fourteen years of this activity, depending on the species and the weather conditions, the young plant finally manages to push its leaves up into the light. Common Spotteds are one of the most common orchids, but they're far from common in this agricultural landscape, so the sprinkling that appears across the Meadow is one of the floral highlights of the year.

As the summer moves on and the vegetation grows higher, the flowers need to raise their heads on tall stiff stems, or thin wiry ones that climb and clamber. There are big spreads of creamy foam when the Meadow Sweet comes into bloom, scattered with the tall spires of Purple Loosestrife. Greater Birdsfoot-trefoil, Tufted Vetch, Yarrow, Knapweed – all are flowers that reveal an ancient grassland. The big umbrella-heads of Angelica are a favourite of mine, always covered with throngs of busy insects. A rich flora is the basis for a rich web of wildlife and this is usually a good spot for butterflies – Orange Tip, Green-veined White, Meadow Brown and Ringlet. The dense cover is well used by many of the farm's inhabitants. I sometimes put up a Snipe, now and again a Fox or a Hare, and once I very nearly walked on a Reed Bunting's nest.

Wildflowers in the Meadow

Barren Strawberry	*Potentilla sterilis*
Bluebell	*Hyacinthoides non-scripta*
Brooklime	*Veronica beccabunga*
Bugle	*Ajuga reptans*
Bush Vetch	*Vicia sepium*
Common Figwort	*Scrophularia nodosa*
Common Knapweed	*Centaurea nigra*
Common Sorrel	*Rumex acetosa*
Common Spotted-orchid	*Dactylorhiza fuchsii*
Common Valerian	*Valeriana officinalis*
Cuckooflower	*Cardamine pratensis*
Dandelion	*Taraxicum vulgaris*
Dog-violet	*Viola riviniana*
Early-purple Orchid	*Orchis mascula*
Foxglove	*Digitalis purpurea*
Greater Bird's-foot-trefoil	*Lotus uliginosus*
Greater Stichwort	*Stellaria holostea*
Hedge Woundwort	*Stachys sylvatica*
Herb-Robert	*Geranium robertianum*
Lesser Celandine	*Ranunculus ficaria*
Marsh Ragwort	*Senecio aquaticus*
Marsh-bedstraw	*Galium palustre*
Marsh-marigold	*Caltha palustris*
Meadow Buttercup	*Ranunculus acris*
Meadow Vetchling	*Lathyrus pratensis*
Meadowsweet	*Filipendula ulmaria*
Pignut	*Conopodium majus*
Primrose	*Primula vulgaris*
Purple-loosestrife	*Lythrum salicaria*
Ragged-Robin	*Lychnis flos-cuculi*
Slender St John's-wort	*Hypericum pulchrum*
Tufted Vetch	*Vicia cracca*
Wild Angelica	*Angelica sylvestris*
Wood-sorrel	*Oxalis acetosella*
Yarrow	*Achillea millefolium*
Yellow Iris	*Iris pseudacorus*

Prickly Customers

S itting in the sun at the front door one summer a few years ago, I slowly became aware of a steady peaceful snoring. I was surprised to discover that it was coming from a pile of old leaves, right beside the doorstep. Our garden is not exactly noted for its tidiness. Carefully separating the leaves, I found a dozing Hedgehog, totally relaxed in its daytime nest, not even bothering to curl up tighter when I intruded.

A completely curled Hedgehog is an amazing thing! When it needs to roll up for protection, it tightens a muscle around the edge of its coat which acts like a drawstring and pulls everything inside. It also has the trick of being able to point its 5000 inch-long spines in different directions, creating something like a coat of barbed wire. There's not a chink to be seen anywhere. Badgers can breach these defences with some effort, but most predators leave Hedgehogs strictly alone. Foxes have been known to push the prickly ball into water to make it uncurl – but this tactic may not work, for Hedgehogs are surprisingly good swimmers.

Daytime snoozing in summer is very different from winter hibernation. For the best part of five months the Hedgehog sinks into a deep cold sleep, always in a solitary nest, living off its store of fat, and with a drop in body temperature from 35 degrees to 4 degrees celsius. Now and again in warmer weather it may come round briefly and slip out for a feed. I've seen one walking across the garden in the middle of December. But many of them don't survive the winter. It's reckoned that a young Hedgehog must weigh at least 1 lb (450 grams) to have any hope of coming through.

Hedgehog courtship can be a very noisy affair. Several times I've been woken up in the middle of the night by the sound effects from the garden. Someone claims to have detected a hedgehog vocabulary of 25 different squeals, squeaks, grunts and snorts! As soon as they've mated, the pair go their separate ways and the female raises the family single-handed.

This solitary lifestyle works well for Hedgehogs and they have changed very little in 15 million years. Our own early ancestors emerged less than three million years ago, and modern Humans have been around for only about 50,000 years. Hedgehogs with their primitive bodies and small brains have never bothered to defend territories or form complicated social groups because they never needed to. What has made them such brilliant survivors is that amazing coat of armour.

Hares and Rabbits

When we were children we used to try to remember to say "hares" or "rabbits" first thing in the morning on the first day of the month. "Hares" if you wanted the month to go fast, and "rabbits" if you wanted it to go slowly – obviously important in the school holidays. Superstitions around Hares and Rabbits are widespread all over the world, apparently linked with the image on the Moon, which some might see as a face, but many more see as a rabbit or hare shape – with the two long ears on the right-hand side.

Ancient folklore from places as far apart as China, India, North and South America, Egypt and Southern Africa had stories connecting Hares or Rabbits with the Moon, and also with themes of death and resurrection. Ever since Humans began to watch and wonder at the night sky, they saw the same story unfolding every month – the moon slowly waxing and waning and disappearing. And then there were three dark nights with no Moon at all until the thin crescent slid into sight again. It's hardly surprising that the earliest calendars measured time in lunar months, and no coincidence that we still calculate the date of Easter in relation to the Moon's cycle. Your chocolate Easter Bunny has more to it than meets the eye.

Coming back down to Earth, Hares and Rabbits may look similar but they have rather different lifestyles, and very different histories in Ireland. The Irish Hare has been around for a long time. A specimen found in Waterford has been dated at over 28,000 years old, making it one of our longest-established mammals.

It's a unique sub-species of the Mountain or Blue Hare found in northern parts of the world, but while most Mountain Hares do live in upland areas, our Hare is found across the whole country.

Brown Hares are a separate species, widespread in lowland Britain, which were brought over to several locations in Ireland in the 1800s. Up until the 1980s we occasionally saw a few of these around the farm, though not in recent years. But Irish Hares have always been well settled here, and seem to have a particular liking for the Croft Plantation. I often have great views of one sitting up like a statue among the trees, or loping off with that graceful long-legged action. But only once have I managed to come across one of their "mad March" mating games.

Rabbits are not native animals, coming originally from Southern Europe. First records of their presence in Ireland date from the twelfth century, when they were introduced as a source of meat and pelts, and provided with enclosed and well-protected warrens. Gradually they escaped and spread and by 1600 they were common all over the country. By the middle of the last century they had become a serious pest in many areas, which led to the drastic and questionable solution of control by disease and the introduction of myxomatosis, which very quickly wiped out 99% of the rabbit population. Since then they have made a steady comeback, and although there are occasional outbreaks of the disease, most animals now survive.

Around the farm at present their population seems to be particularly healthy! They have several main strongholds, one of which is well positioned next to the vegetable garden. Early this year one even made a neat burrow right inside my poly-tunnel. Over several days I filled in the hole each morning, and the following night it was opened up again. Eventually I decided to turn the hose down into the burrow to make the interior a bit less comfortable, but got quite a surprise when a whole family of five beautiful baby Rabbits popped out, slightly damp but extremely lively. And believe it or not, it was Easter Sunday morning!

Air Show with Soundtrack

I n the early 2000s there was a new song to be heard around the farm – a rather wild and exotic sound compared with the familiar songbird chorus. Lapwings are mostly found in wide open spaces – saltmarshes and mudflats around coastal estuaries, and great expanses of slobland. In winter when flocks pour over here from mainland Europe, Lapwing numbers can reach up to 200,000 - by far the highest national total of all the wading birds. In spring they move to breeding territories far and wide across northern Europe, and many also nest in Ireland, especially where there's a good mixture of damp grassland and arable fields. But the Irish breeding population has been dwindling fast in recent years, and I'd never known them to nest in this locality.

So there was great excitement when a pair of these beautiful birds turned up and proceeded to set up their territory in a nearby field, with the nest site right out in the middle. Since then there have been a few pairs around every summer, and in the last few years we've had two pairs in fields beside the garden, so we are enjoying a grandstand view of the spectacular flight display. The male can put on his show at any time of day, even late at night, and it lasts for maybe five or ten minutes before he settles down again. The distinctive flapping flight on broad rounded wings is what gives him his name. He patrols up and down the field, calling repeatedly, swerving and tilting from side to side, showing the dark upper wing and then the clear black and white underwing, sometimes soaring high and then plunging down the sky. When he comes close, you can hear the strange throbbing sound that comes from the vibration of his wings.

His song attracts as much attention as his fancy flight. A Lapwing's normal call is a simple "pee-weet" which has given it its other name of Peewit, but the mating call is a loud penetrating "pee-oo-weet-weet-weet – pee-oo-weet", which can echo across several fields and is unmistakable. He's also an unmistakable figure when he lands, standing out in the middle of the field with shining dark green mantle and long curling crest.

Until they started nesting here, my main experience of Lapwings had been watching the swirling flight of the huge winter flocks around the Swilly Estuary, often mixed with Golden Plover – also a great spectacle, but a long-distance one. Having them as next-door neighbours all summer is something else entirely.

A Bird in the Hand

Whatever about the Lapwing aerobatics and the usual entertainment provided by the visiting Swallows and Flycatchers, in the summer of 2007 it was the garden's resident Robin that completely stole the show. It had started back in February with porridge oats on the doorstep, and this Robin was so friendly that it wasn't long until he was taking them from my hand. By the beginning of March he was flying down to land on my fingers, anywhere around the garden, so I had to keep a mobile oat supply in my pocket.

He was usually waiting for me in the morning, and often sat close by and sang when he had finished eating. Sometimes this was his normal loud song, but now and again it was a strange little twittering, so faint that it could only be heard right beside him. Apparently this "sub-song" is produced by various bird species, but the reason for it is still much of a mystery. It's not just a private language for use between mates, for often the mate is nowhere nearby. It really sounded as if he was talking to himself. He actually sang a few times while still perched on my hand – a real thrill.

By the middle of April he had a mate in tow, but she kept very much in the background, and came down to feed on the doorstep only after I went inside. A big part of his courtship involved presenting her with items of food and this soon included oats as well as insects. On 6th May I found their nest, in thick ivy on an old shed, and both of them were feeding young. They hunted steadily all day, ferrying insects and grubs to the nest, and any time I was working in the garden he was close at hand. I saw him bite the head off a large grub and eat that himself, before taking the remainder to the nest. I was quite surprised when he started feeding the young ones on porridge oats as well – taking about a dozen oats at a time and often coming straight back for more. When they left the nest he continued to feed at least three of them for about two weeks, and I was able to find where they were hiding when they got their oat deliveries. The record number of continuous trips between my hand and the young ones was fourteen

By the beginning of June the family was independent and his life became less hectic. He could still pop up at any time of day looking for a snack, and when the door was open he often came into the house and chirped to let me know that he was there. He became so relaxed that he sometimes perched on my fingers on one leg, with the other tucked up. And he once took a very lengthy bath in a dish of water right beside me. Being so up close and personal with a wild bird and sharing the tiny details of his life was a remarkable experience, and full of surprises. A couple of times he started retching and brought up a little black pellet of undigested bits of insects. Producing pellets was something that I'd associated with birds of prey which eat much larger items, and I hadn't realized that some small birds do this as well. Another day he had something very like a fit of sneezing for about a minute.

As expected, our relationship came to an abrupt ending. On 3rd August he was around as usual, and came to be fed at least three times – and the next day he was gone. I searched for him around nearby fields but there was no sign of him. Very soon there was a fresh new Robin patrolling his territory around the front door – maybe even one of his own offspring, so diligently fed on porridge oats.

Old Friends

Every field on the farm has a name, and each one has its own personality. They differ in size and in their "lie of the land" and have different views from their vantage points, but it's the wide variety of the hedgerows, and the trees along their margins, that really gives them their character. All the thousands of trees in the plantations are youngsters to be carefully reared and proudly watched as they grow, but the mature hedgerow trees around the farm are more like old friends.

Take the Front Field, for instance, just across from the house. It has the usual range of Ash and Sycamore, but also two fine Copper Beeches on the roadside, the only two Oak trees on the farm apart from all the new plantings, and further along the same side, a group of elegant Wild Cherries. At the opposite side there are two ancient Crabapple trees, and a long line of shimmering Aspens which tremble with the slightest breeze – you can sometimes hear the rustle from right across the field.

The little hilly Mullen field has the best collection of Hazel bushes and the tallest Cherry tree on the farm. The riverbank has its fringe of Alder and impressive Crack Willows, and a secluded corner with the remains of an old wallstead, known as Francie's Garden, has a small gathering of wild Plum trees. You can tell that there was once a garden here as a lovely spread of Snowdrops manages to raise its head every spring, in spite of many years of nibbling by sheep.

Sycamores used to be planted around farm premises for their valuable shade and shelter, and the couple growing close together at the back of the yard provide an excellent wide umbrella. The largest and most ancient-looking trees on the farm are also Sycamores, one along the lane having a girth of fourteen feet. It's been quite hollow for years but still stands firm.

Also on the lane we used to have a row of magnificent old Elms which have been falling victim, one by one, to Dutch Elm disease over the last twenty years. The disease is caused by a fungus carried by a tiny bark beetle which attacks only Elm trees, and there's no way of stopping its spread. A young Elm will survive to the age of about thirty, but it will then almost surely be attacked.

The older trees in the Back Field are mostly Ash, and one of them has to be rated as the most remarkable of any on the farm. It's probably about 200 years old with a huge solid trunk which sits on top of a rocky outcrop overlooking one of the ponds. Two great arms (or legs?) of root stretch down across the rock to frame a little pool which is fed by a spring that never dries, even in the driest summer, and which feeds on into the pond. I have no idea if this was ever regarded as a holy well or spring, but it certainly would have been a good candidate.

Autumn Aspens

Bats in the Chimney

For several years now, a tall chimney at the back of the house has been used as summer breeding quarters by a large colony of bats. Every evening around dusk there's a great chorus of twittering which can be heard clearly from below, and a stream of bats start to pop out of a tiny chink in the outside plaster and shoot off like darts for their night's hunting. Now and again I'm up early enough around dawn to see dozens of them circling the chimney before popping in again. I usually start to notice them in May, and by September they have all moved away to more secluded sites for their winter hibernation.

Ireland has ten different bat species and we've identified several of them around the farm. They are such elusive and nocturnal creatures that they've always been hard to study, but the job has been made a lot easier with the invention of the bat-detector. This is a gadget which picks up their high-pitched flight calls which echo back to them from everything in their path, giving them a complete image of their surroundings through sound. They can pinpoint tiny insects and even tell what direction these are moving in. Each species has a different-pitched call, with its own pattern of clicks and squeaks. Just a few years ago it was discovered that the smallest and most common one, the Pipistrelle, had two distinct calls, and it turned out to be two quite separate species. We have always known that our chimney colony is of Pipistrelles, but recently were pleased to confirm that we have both types in residence. We also regularly see a much larger shape flitting past which has got to be a Leisler's – the biggest Irish bat which weighs about twenty grams in autumn just before hibernation, compared with eight grams for a Pipistrelle. There are also Brown

Long-eared Bats around, for we once found one in the house – unmistakable, with ears three-quarters the length of its head and body together.

Bats are not often seen by day but twice I've been surprised to see what I assume to be a Daubenton's or Water Bat flitting over the river in bright sunlight. For several minutes it darted back and forward across the water, dipping down to skim the surface, showing off its brown furry coat in the sun. A bat flits so fast that it's not easy to follow with binoculars, and even when I managed to focus directly on a spot where it touched the water, it was impossible to see whether it was picking up insects from the surface or just having a drink. It can hook insects with its feet, or scoop them up with its tail.

All Irish bats are insect-eaters and the various species specialize in different types and sizes of insect, which helps to avoid too much competition. The Leisler's Bat takes things like moths and daddy-longlegs, while a Pipistrelle can polish off 3000 midges and mosquitoes in one night. But the bats themselves can become another link in the food-chain. One year we were able to watch some remarkable behaviour which was a sort of fascinating horror show. The local Sparrowhawk had discovered the Pipistrelles in the chimney, and it would take up its position in good time each evening. It perched just above the entrance chink, now and again leaning over to peer into the hole, occasionally taking to the wing and pecking impatiently at the spot – not apparently the best of tactics to encourage the bats to come out! But eventually they had to take their chance. They pop out so fast that it took three or four attempts before the hawk made a successful strike. Generally it took its catch away, but twice I watched it sit up on the chimney and consume the victim on the spot. It was a vivid demonstration of Nature red in tooth and claw. But the Sparrowhawk didn't have everything its own way. One night as I was watching, the local Long-eared Owl must have taken exception to this daylight predator encroaching on his night-time domain, for it swooped across the yard, lunged at the Sparrowhawk, and chased it off.

The Butterfly Bushes

Each summer a wave of exotic insects moves northwards from north Africa and southern Europe, but there's a big variation in numbers from year to year, and big differences in how far they manage to travel. Over the last few years the effects of climate change are beginning to be felt, and sightings of these rare visitors are becoming much more regular and widespread.

The Hummingbird Hawk-moth is an amazing little character which we had watched several times in Spain and France, but we had never seen it in Ireland or Britain, so you can imagine the scene, one sunny July afternoon in 2003, when one turned up in our back garden! We were just checking the butterflies on the Buddleia bushes when this small mouse-grey creature with white-speckled rear and whirring orange wings zoomed into view. What makes this Hawk-moth so spectacular is its enormously long tongue, or proboscis, slightly longer than its own body, which it uses to suck nectar. It hovers some distance from the flower, very like an American Hummingbird, holding its body perfectly still between the blur of wings, deftly probing each floret with what looks just like a fishing rod and line.

Peacock

Since that famous occasion there has been a steady trickle of Hummingbird Hawk-moth sightings in Donegal, and we've spotted a couple more around the garden and elsewhere. Migrant butterflies are also turning up in much greater numbers, especially Red Admirals and Painted Ladies. The influx of Painted Ladies in the summer of 2009, when thousands poured in all across the country over a few days, was one of the most amazing butterfly spectacles of recent times. I hadn't heard that it was happening, and could hardly believe what I was seeing when I met a stream of these rare visitors moving across the Back Field.

Lots of different garden plants are recommended for attracting moths and butterflies, including Sedum, Tobacco-plant and Hemp Agrimony. But it's Buddleia that really deserves its reputation as the "butterfly bush" as it's such a reliable magnet, especially for all the beautiful Vanessid butterflies, but also for the less showy members of the White and Brown families, and big numbers of moths, bees and hoverflies. The big sprawling bushes come in different colours – purple, white, yellow, and shades of pink and mauve. We have eight of them around the garden, set in different corners to catch the sun at different times of day, and I do a regular patrol to see what might be turning up.

The Vanessids include the migrant Red Admiral and Painted Lady, and also the resident Small Tortoiseshell and Peacock – the only two butterflies which hibernate in Ireland in their adult form. All other resident species spend the winter as a pupa or caterpillar. Small Tortoiseshells often come into the house in August and September, looking for a suitable spot to tuck themselves away until the spring. A favourite hiding place is inside the folds of curtains. One year in October I was taking down some curtains and found seventeen of them, fast asleep. I carefully transferred them to a box in a cool room, and looked in now and again through the winter to see how they were. Not a sign of life or movement. They looked just like bits of dead leaf.

Red Admiral

One day in April I found one fluttering on the window and let it out. The weather wasn't great but anything which is just coming out of hibernation needs food fast. A few days later it was warm and bright and I decided the time had come for the others to waken up. Still none had moved when I set the box out in the sun, but within a couple of minutes the wings were starting to vibrate, and one-by-one they opened out to flash their beautiful colours and fly off into the spring. Only two of them were dead. Having kept an eye on them for six months, it did feel good to see the motionless forms coming back to life, settling on flowers, absorbing the sun. And within five minutes some of them were already into the mating game, sizing one another up as they circled around in twos and threes, spiraling high into the sky.

A Lawn for Life

A wildlife-friendly garden should have a maximum of nature-watching and a minimum of work! We have always applied this principle very rigorously to the management of our lawn. It does get cut when necessary, but it never gets treated with any sort of artificial fertilizer or herbicide or moss-killer, and the only fertilizing it gets from above is from the falling leaves in autumn. The soil underneath is also kept in good heart by the army of earthworms and invertebrates, and by the rich variety of fungi.

I can never understand why so many people panic at the sight of moss on their lawn. We have a nice variety of moss species which are beautiful in themselves, rich and soft underfoot, perfectly mowable, and fresh and green all year round. And then there are the wildflowers. At different times of the year we adjust the cutting-height of the mower to accommodate spreads of Daisies or Selfheal or White Clover, and in May the lawn has its blue period when parts of it mist over with Slender Speedwell.

Citrine Waxcap

We keep a broad area of long grass around the edge for the taller hay-meadow flowers like Knapweed and Birdsfoot-trefoil and Ox-eye Daisy, and this gets cut just once or twice a year. All this plant diversity draws in insects and other mini-beasts and the birds that feed on them. We never need to aerate the soil with spiky instruments for the earthworms do that job as well.

In late summer and early autumn the lawn becomes a demonstration of mushroom magic! For weeks there's a constant stream of new arrivals which provide a fresh treasure-hunt every morning. The fungi come in a whole variety of colours and textures, mostly in the classic mushroom or toadstool shape, but there are also various cups and saucers, clusters of long worm-like fingers and tiny pin-heads. The big eye-catchers are the Waxcaps. We now have six different species of these – gleaming knuckles in bright colours, slimy to the touch. They're reckoned to be good indicators of old natural grassland. First on the scene are usually the Pink Waxcaps which develop into elegant parasols with upturned wavy edges. The Citrine, Meadow and Parrot Waxcaps, as shown in the photographs, demonstrate their brilliant variety.

By the time the fungal activity is dying away with the first frosts, the lawn will have its first sprinkling of autumn leaves and beechmast, and it becomes a happy hunting ground all winter for everything from Woodpigeons to tiny Coal Tits.

Meadow Waxcap

Parrot Waxcap

Pink Waxcap

A New Orchard

few years ago our oldest Bramley Apple tree finally gave up the struggle. For several seasons it had been dropping branches and getting thinner on top, but was still producing some fine apples, until a winter storm finished it off. Bramley is the biggest name in cooking apples and the most widely-grown variety in commercial orchards, and most old gardens would have had one or two of them. Remarkably, all of these are descended from a single tree in a garden in Nottinghamshire, reckoned to be 200 years old and still producing fruit.

Apples have been cultivated and adapted for human use for thousands of years, and constant selection and hybridization have produced thousands of different varieties. Most of them have a very complex genetic make-up and don't breed true. Pips from one tree will produce all sorts and sizes of offspring, so apple breeders have to propagate their trees by grafting buds on to suitable seedling trees, or "root stock". A wild Crabapple can of course still be grown from a pip.

Our garden still had half a dozen healthy trees, both cookers and eaters, but the loss of our huge old Bramley prompted us to think about creating something like a new orchard. That meant getting in touch with the Irish Seed Savers Association, based at Scariff in Co. Clare. This group has been making a huge effort since the 1990s to find and propagate old traditional varieties of Irish apple, and they now have over 140 different types thriving in their orchards, with 90 varieties offered for sale. Just looking through their Apple Catalogue or website is an inspiration in itself, with details of where the different varieties came from, and good descriptions of the fruit. We chose seven trees, all eating apples and most of Irish origin, which ripen at slightly different times. Now seven years old, six of them are producing fruit, and we're enjoying discovering their different textures and flavours.

Old varieties which were developed for our mild and damp climate
tend to have good resistance to problems like scab, mildew and
canker, so shouldn't need any spraying with pesticides. The long-term
survival of these great traditional apples depends on as many trees as
possible finding their way back to where they came from – ordinary
back gardens.

Hedgerow Harvest

The edge of a hedge is really the border between two different habitats – and where two habitats meet, you usually find the greatest variety of wildlife. A big mature hedgerow is where you find the plants and animals of the woodland edge mixing with those which live in grassland or arable fields, together with some species which need a bit of both. So the mesh of hedgerows spread across the countryside is a vital network of nature reserves, acting as highways for animal life to travel along, and plant life to disperse itself. Half-a-mile of hedge can support over 30 pairs of nesting birds.

A good hedgerow is also a well-stocked and highly-organised larder. From early spring through to late summer, the shrubby plants take it in turns to do their flowering so that they share out the services of the insect pollinators – which suits the insects as well.

From the first flush of white flowers on the bare Blackthorn bushes
in early April, you can follow the trail of blossom around the farm
through the weeks – Hawthorn, Gorse, Cherry, Plum, Crabapple,
Rowan, Elder, Guelder Rose, Honeysuckle, Wild Rose, Bramble. A
useful yardstick for measuring the age and value of any hedge is the
number of different trees and woody shrubs along its length. The best
one on the farm has eighteen species which means that it's likely that
it was originally connected to ancient woodland.

In contrast to the succession in their flowering, most of the shrubs
in autumn tend to do their fruiting all together – just when the birds
need a good supply of fruits and berries to build them up for the
winter. The exceptions are Holly and Ivy, the Christmas specials,
which come on stream later. Ivy has the most unusual time-table of
them all, which makes it a real life-saver for wildlife in winter.

From November through to January mature plants are covered with sprays of yellow florets, rich in nectar and pollen, and a magnet for any insects which are still around, including late-flying moths. The dark chocolate-coloured berries ripen through to March, and although these are not very succulent, they fill a hungry gap for many birds and small mammals.

There's a long running debate about the merits of Ivy. Some people really resent the graceful lines of a tree disappearing inside a thick green shroud, and maintain that a heavy load of Ivy must be doing some sort of damage. Certainly, when it has reached the stage of developing a huge crown of its own, high up in the tree canopy, it will increase the chances of that tree coming down in a storm, so it's wise to cut through the ivy stems at the base and let it die back, particularly if the tree is next to a roadside. But in most cases Ivy is doing the tree no harm. It has its own root system, and the suckers that attach it to the tree are just for support, not drawing any nourishment from its host. So except for prominent trees in the garden, we are happy to let it climb to a good height, and in winter when colour is draining away from the countryside, it's good to have a few splashes of bright green to cheer the scene. And apart from the value of its flowers and berries as a food source, the thick glossy foliage is  obviously a vital shelter for all sorts of wildlife, and a roost and nest site for many birds. Farm animals too are known to be wise to Ivy's qualities, and many a sick cow or sheep has been coaxed back to food with a bit of Ivy when all else failed.

Wild Cherries

Guelder Rose

Welcoming Foxes

L ate summer and early autumn is the best time for meeting
Foxes. The young ones are beginning to enjoy their
independence and explore their surroundings, and they haven't
fully realized that Humans are not to be trusted. I often come across
two or three siblings on the move together, especially on late
evenings in a freshly-cut silage or arable field where there's a nice
fresh supply of tasty tit-bits. It's usually not too long before they
decide that it's time for a game.

It's very sad that the condemnation and persecution of Foxes still
persists in so many places. Surely it's time that these beautiful
intelligent animals should be allowed to live in peace and fulfill their
natural role in the countryside. By far the greatest part of their diet
is made up of rabbits, rats and mice, and they also depend on small
items like beetles and earthworms. Foxy visits to hen-runs are of
course the stuff of legend, but the danger is often exaggerated. In
many years of leaving my hen-house door open through the night in
summer, my hens suffered only two fox raids. After that, however,
I did keep the door closed!

Foxes will scavenge on dead animals, but very rarely take live lambs.
On two occasions I've been interested to watch a large Fox wandering
among a flock of sheep. Some were grazing and others lying down,
and I was surprised to see that none of them even bothered to raise
their heads as the Fox walked close by. Clearly these animals had
no inbuilt fear of Foxes. And yet the same flock would have
immediately bunched together in panic if a dog appeared in their
field – even something the size of a Yorkshire Terrier.

Killing Foxes is also quite unnecessary to keep their population in check, for they do that themselves by adjusting their breeding rate to available territory and food supply. The classic example is what happened in Glenveagh National Park. Under the previous regime the Foxes were culled every year, but once the estate became a National Park the animals were protected, and Fox numbers remained exactly the same. In Britain, fox-hunting enthusiasts often maintain that without their so-called sport the countryside would be overrun with Foxes. But during the foot-and-mouth crisis in 2001 when hunting was banned for a year, detailed surveys by the Mammal Society showed that their numbers did not increase, and even decreased in some areas.

One of my best fox experiences was a couple of years ago when I was watching a pair of young ones playing in the Back Field. Eventually they noticed me, and one of them slipped off quickly into the hedge. But the other one came closer and closer to investigate, and when it was just a few feet away, sat down and stared. And then it started to bark – a sharp howling yelp that got louder and louder and more indignant, and went on for several minutes. The message was clear. This was his playground, and I had no business being there to spoil the fun. It was lovely to see this little creature so full of confidence, so much at home. I took the hint and left.

Close Encounters with Stoats

Fox entertainment is fairly frequent, but sightings of Stoats around the farm are few and far between. However, the two occasions when I've had close encounters with these feisty little animals were certainly memorable. The first was in the Croft Plantation. I had noticed for several days a neat round hole in the middle of one of the paths, and decided to find out how deep it was by inserting a long bendy twig. With my face close to the hole and the twig just a few inches inside, there was suddenly a most ear-piercing squeal and out popped a sharp little furry face. I must have jumped several feet! This was a very angry Stoat and it continued to shout at me for some seconds before it ducked inside. I waited to see what would happen, and sure enough, out it came again to get a better look at me. We scrutinized one another for maybe a minute before it finally disappeared.

The other occasion was when I found a small one, apparently dead, on the kitchen floor. Our now elderly cat was a more lively spark in those days, and there she was, sitting smugly beside her trophy. I picked up the long slender body, golden brown above and silky white beneath, and it was still warm but completely limp. And then I suddenly realized that it was breathing! Wild animals in distress should be kept in a warm dark place so I put it carefully in a box, but before I could decide what to

do next there was a fierce scrabbling and shrill squeaking inside the box and it was clear that this animal was very much alive. When I released it outside, it was off like a dart.

But the drama wasn't over. A few minutes later I heard loud squeals from the garden – Sheba had slipped out and managed to catch it again! This time she had it in her clutches on top of a pillar and wasn't going to let go. But I had the bright idea of using the garden hose, and a quick squirt did the trick – the cat jumped down in one direction and the Stoat in the other, and I didn't see it again.

This was obviously a young animal, for Stoats are famous for being tough fighters and often kill Rabbits up to five times their own weight. If this had been an adult, Sheba might have had a rather different adventure.

Birds regularly found on the farm

Blackbird	*Turdus merula*
Blackcap	*Sylvia atricapilla*
Blue Tit	*Parus caeruleus*
Bullfinch	*Pyrrhula pyrrhula*
Buzzard	*Buteo buteo*
Chaffinch	*Fringilla coelebs*
Chiffchaff	*Phylloscopus collybita*
Coal Tit	*Parus ater*
Collared Dove	*Streptopelia decaocto*
Dipper	*Cinclus cinclus*
Dunnock	*Prunella modularis*
Feral Pigeon	*Columba livia*
Fieldfare	*Turdus pilaris*
Goldcrest	*Regulus regulus*
Goldfinch	*Carduelis carduelis*
Great Tit	*Parus major*
Greenfinch	*Carduelis chloris*
Grey Wagtail	*Motacilla cinerea*
Heron	*Ardea cinerea*
Hooded Crow	*Corvus corone*
House Martin	*Delichon urbica*
House Sparrow	*Passer domesticus*
Jackdaw	*Corvus monedula*
Jay	*Garrulus glandarius*
Kingfisher	*Alcedo atthis*
Lapwing	*Vanellus vanellus*
Lesser Black-backed Gull	*Larus fuscus*
Long-eared Owl	*Asio otus*
Long-tailed Tit	*Aegithalos caudatus*
Magpie	*Pica pica*

Mallard	*Anas platyrhynchos*
Mistle Thrush	*Turdus viscivorus*
Moorhen	*Gallinula chloropus*
Pheasant	*Phasianus colchicus*
Pied Wagtail	*Motacilla alba yarrellii*
Raven	*Corvus corax*
Redpoll	*Carduelis flammea*
Redwing	*Turdus iliacus*
Reed Bunting	*Emberiza schoeniclus*
Robin	*Erithacus rubecula*
Rook	*Corvus frugilegus*
Sand Martin	*Riparia riparia*
Siskin	*Carduelis spinus*
Snipe	*Gallinago gallinago*
Song Thrush	*Turdus philomelos*
Sparrowhawk	*Accipiter nisus*
Spotted Flycatcher	*Muscicapa striata*
Starling	*Sturnus vulgaris*
Stock Dove	*Columba oenas*
Swallow	*Hirundo rustica*
Teal	*Anas crecca*
Treecreeper	*Certhia familiaris*
Willow Warbler	*Phylloscopus trochilus*
Woodcock	*Scolopax rusticola*
Woodpigeon	*Columba palumbus*
Wren	*Troglodytes troglodytes*

The Winter Thrushes

I t always comes as a nice surprise even though it's half-expected – the first flock of Fieldfare or Redwing in the autumn is as symbolic as the first Swallow in the spring. It's another big turning point in the annual flow of birdlife, and a comforting signal that the natural world is doing business as usual. Out on the coast the winter migrants arrive in their hundreds and thousands – geese and swans and ducks and waders – but here in inland farming country it's these colourful members of the Thrush family that sound the warning that winter is on the way.

Fieldfare and Redwing breed up in Scandinavia and the north of Central Europe and they start to move south and westwards in autumn, using up the berry crop as they go. They usually arrive on the farm here sometime during November, and stay around for most of the winter, feeding in the Hawthorn hedges and Ash trees and down on the stubble fields. The flocks have a very distinctive flicker as they flit along, from the red flanks and underwings of the Redwings and the silvery underwings of the Fieldfare.

I often come across a large flock of them in our Back Field, and a few winters ago I noticed a curious thing – the Hawthorn berries were dwindling steadily all around the field, except for those on three large bushes which were still so heavily laden that they were shining bright red from quite a distance. The mystery was soon solved – there was a Mistle Thrush on guard.

These large resident Thrushes are well-known for staking out their claim to a good berry supply and driving off all intruders that come anywhere near. As long as weather permits they continue with their normal diet of worms and grubs and insects, foraging about on the ground. But when a hard frost sets in and they're not able to probe the soil, the well-guarded berry store comes in very handy. That at least is the plan, and it often works, but the larder is not short of invaders and the biggest threat often comes from those close relations from the far north. In a spell of really hard winter weather even the toughest Mistle Thrush may not be able to hold out against a hungry gang of several dozen.

Fieldfare and Redwing are generally wild and wary and not likely to turn up in the garden, but now and again during a long period of frost or snow I've managed to entice a few of them very close to the doorstep when I laid on a supply of windfall apples. Their Irish names show that these birds have always been seen as symbols of harsh weather and wild winter – the Fieldfare is "Sacan", the frost bird, and the Redwing is "Deargan Sneachta", the red bird of the snow.

Web Sites

There's nearly always a particular day in autumn, a still and misty morning, when the hedgerows and plantation paths have suddenly become display galleries for the wonders of the web. Spiders are living close to us all the time in vast numbers, but we hardly notice them. Apart, that is, from the large black ones around the house, which in my case get evicted very smartly!

In autumn the spiders and their webs are at their largest, but it takes a misty morning to bring the astonishing creations to light, when every strand of silk is marked out with shining droplets. Gorse bushes especially are often festooned with huge numbers of hammock or dome-shaped webs – beautifully elaborate crisscross structures, suspended and braced by single strands attached to surrounding foliage. They are truly wonderful feats of engineering.

The other main type of web design is the classic round orb with spokes from the centre, filled in with a neat geometric spiral, generally created by Garden Spiders. Most are saucer-sized and some are as big as dinner plates, deftly positioned between twigs and stems, sometimes spanning right across the plantation path. Catch one of these in the sunlight and it becomes a curtain of sparkling dewdrops, glinting with rainbow colours. I sometimes have to take a detour to avoid vandalising such works of art, but at least it's a comfort to know that when a web gets damaged, the spider can eat the silk so that it doesn't go to waste – a very efficient internal recycling system.

Another type of web display is the shimmering sheet of gossamer which can cover a whole field on warmer autumn days, especially just after a cold snap. This happens when hordes of tiny Money Spiders have taken to the air to disperse themselves to new locations. Their numbers have been counted at over a million to the acre. When weather conditions are just right, they climb up to the tips of nearby stems and each one spins out a strand of silk long enough to carry its own weight. Then it simply lets go and allows itself to float free and waft along like a kite, often drifting for many miles before it comes to rest. I sometimes notice big numbers of silken strands floating past, but the tiny travellers are far too small to see.

The Bird on the Bark

Treecreepers are well named. These remarkable little resident birds are not widely recognized, although they're actually fairly common in any area with a reasonable number of mature trees. I often see them around the garden and hedgerows, and increasingly in the plantations, particularly in winter when the branches are bare.

Treecreepers are so superbly adapted to living on the trunks and branches of large trees that you hardly ever see one anywhere else. The first thing you're likely to notice is what looks like a small mouse scuttling up a trunk, always working its way upwards from the bottom, often moving in a spiral around the tree and running along upside down on the underside of branches. Its whole body is designed as a precision instrument for prising food items out of cracks and fissures in the bark – insects and other mini-beasts and their eggs. Large feet with sharp claws help it to cling on tightly, stiff tail feathers brace the body against the tree to get more leverage, but most of all, the long curved beak with needle-point can delicately pick the tiniest mite out of the tightest crack.

And so they live out their whole life around tree trunks. They roost and nest in chinks behind the bark, or in a thick growth of ivy. All ornithological reference books mention their well-known habit of carving out little roosting places in the thick soft bark of the Wellingtonia tree, a large ornamental conifer from California which wasn't introduced into Ireland or Britain until the mid-1800s. I've seen a few of these neat oval excavations, about the size of a half hard-boiled egg, in Wellingtonias in parks, but have never come across a bird sitting in one.

However, a few summers ago I noticed that a half-rotten Crack Willow on the riverbank at the bottom of the Millennium Plantation had several suspicious-looking newly-excavated holes, about twelve feet from the ground, and I'd been wondering about them. And then late one evening, there it was! A roosting Treecreeper was snugly fitted into one of the holes, streaky back completely filling it, a perfect camouflage, with tail protruding below and the little curved beak sticking up above. It's obvious that they've always had this hole-carving habit when they can find any wood that's soft enough. But strangely, the only reference that I could find anywhere to Treecreepers excavating any tree other than a Wellingtonia was as far back as 1936.

I saw my bird tucked into one or other of the holes on several further occasions before the end of the summer. But sadly, that particular roost-site is now no more, for the Willow stump came down in a storm the following winter.

Christmas Pheasants

It wasn't exactly a winter wonderland on 25th December, 2004, but there was just about enough snow cover to make it a White Christmas, just enough to draw attention beyond the Christmas tree and out into the garden. And then in the middle of the afternoon the decorations arrived! There was a loud "kutok-kutok" outside the window and we looked out to see two beautiful cock Pheasants strutting about on the snowy lawn, brilliant in their festive colours of red, green and gold.

Pheasants generally manage to go about their business in remarkable privacy, considering their large size, but when the breeding season is getting near, the males seem to throw all caution to the wind, and when you see one parading in his full regalia, you wonder how this flashy character ever manages to hide himself at all. Bright red face mask, dark green peaked hood, and shining cloak of copper coins. The finely-barred tail is as long as the rest of him. His whole style gives a hint of his exotic origins, for Pheasants are not native Irish birds, but were introduced long ago from China and other parts of Asia.

The two on the lawn were so absorbed in their confrontation that they completely ignored the watchers at the window. The slightly larger bird was obviously the dominant male defending his territory, but the younger one wasn't going to give way too easily. For about twenty minutes they displayed and faced up to one another, a ritual dance that was full of aggressive moves, but they never made any actual physical contact. There was a lot of head-ducking and forward dabbing. Sometimes one would move off, but the other quickly followed and they soon engaged again. Now and again they walked along side by side, getting the measure of one another. They finally disappeared under the hedge so we didn't discover who came out on top, but presumably it was the older stronger bird.

As the breeding season advances, the encounters between rival males can sometimes become more violent, but they rarely result in death or serious injury. Most species have developed the art of sorting out their disputes without killing one another. It would seem that Humans are some of the slower learners.

Sleeping Beauties

The classic Seven-spot Ladybird, bright red with black spots, is just one of over twenty different ladybird species found in Ireland. Most are red or yellow with different numbers of spots, some have no spots at all, and some have other markings. They're basically small flying beetles which can travel for several miles using their flimsy hind wings, which are folded neatly away under the hard colourful wing-cases when they land. All of them hibernate through the winter months, usually well out of sight, behind tree bark or house plaster or maybe down the middle of a hollow stem. I had never expected to come across any of them in the middle of winter.

So it was a big surprise one December to discover that some of the young Ash trees in the Millennium Plantation had dozens of clusters of sleeping ladybirds, mostly in groups of ten to twenty, sitting on the bare trunks and branches in full view. On the whole they were clinging to the undersides of branches, but these were small trees and they would have had hardly any protection from wind and rain.

Even more surprising was the fact that they were of a type that we had never seen before – the Orange Ladybird, which is generally quite scarce. They have bright orange wing-cases with sixteen clear white spots – a nice contrast to the familiar red Seven-spot. Needless to say, the remarkable gathering was well watched through the next few months, and the numbers dwindled steadily – from over 600 down to 120 at the last count before they finally dispersed in the spring. How any of them managed to survive in such exposed positions was quite amazing.

We were interested to hear from two couples who live at opposite ends of the county that they had also discovered groups of Orange Ladybirds in their young plantations that same winter. The species must have had some sort of population explosion. In the half-dozen winters since then we have found just a few every year, still sitting out on the bare branches, still in the very same group of Ash trees.

Orange Ladybirds

The Story Continues.....

In 2010, as the Millennium Plantation reached its tenth birthday we felt that we had to keep the sequence going, and another patch of land was planted – rather smaller this time. The ten-year intervals between the plantations have become a very useful illustration of the early stages in the development of a broadleaf woodland. And it's not just the trees themselves. It's been so interesting to see the variety of plant life that has moved in at different times – the mosses and ferns and fungi; the first clumps of Celandine and Bluebell and Golden Saxifrage; the Rosebay Willowherb that appeared from nowhere. We're now seeing the beginnings of natural regeneration as little seedling trees begin to sprout up after thinning.

Every year is a fresh experience with something new to discover, or something to check up on. Will the Jays turn up again in the autumn? How many of the nest boxes will be occupied? Will a new moth species turn up in the trap? The various tree species come into the limelight at different times – the first flush of green in the Birches or the gorgeous variety of autumn colour in the Maples. In mid-winter all the attention is on the Alders when their small woody cone-like fruits, packed with oil-rich seeds, become such a magnet for colourful flocks of tits and finches. Goldfinches and the various Tit species are around all year, but Siskin and Redpoll are a rarer sight, for these spend the summer in upland forests and move down to the lowlands in winter. We hardly ever saw them here before we had the plantations. So far, the main use for the timber thinnings has been for firewood, but we also leave some piles of logs and branches behind to act as shelters for small birds and mammals, and the whole invertebrate community that thrives on rotting wood.

Many groups of foresters and farmers have visited, and we're always hoping that more and more people will discover the pleasures, and good sense, of broadleaf planting. We were delighted in 2005 to win the RDS/Forest Service Forestry Award for Biodiverse Woodlands, and in 2006 to host the launching of that year's competition. It was good to have the wildlife value of our woods affirmed, but we were also very pleased when the judges assured us that the timber value of the trees is very satisfactory as well. Farm plantations have to pay their way, and we would hope that these woods will be managed in years to come with a system of continuous cover. In other words, they would never be clear-felled, but selectively cropped so that there would always be continuity in the habitat and wildlife community. Meanwhile, it's very satisfying now to look down across the valley and see that our little woodlands are making their mark on the landscape.

The story of our time here will hopefully continue to accumulate further chapters, but whatever its length, it will be just another brief episode in the history of this small patch of the Earth. What will it look like in a hundred years' time? Or a thousand? How will it be affected by changes in climate and population and land use? The natural world never ceases to evolve and the cast of characters will change, but I would love to think that the Badgers will still be doing their nightly rounds, and that the summer sky will still be alive with Swallows and Spotted Flycatchers. And with a bit of luck, some of the Oak trees that we planted, or their descendants, might still be standing their ground.